INVESTING FOR TEENS

From Pocket Money to Profits: An Investing Handbook for Teenagers

Bonus: List of Custodial Investment Accounts

Daniel R

TABLE OF CONTENTS

INTRODUCTION

If you are interested in improving your financial future while you're still young, this is the right book for it. You may be trying to figure out how to go about doing it. One of those ways happens to be investing.

As a young person, you have plenty of life ahead of you. Thus, you should consider yourself lucky that you have the best time and opportunity to start investing. You've probably heard your parents say things like "I wish I started this when I was younger".

However, now is the time to avoid that on your own accord. This book will discuss how you can invest while you are still a teenager. The good news is that this will cover the basic information on investing.

Even better - you're not going to learn any of the advanced, complicated stuff that goes with investing. Which means we won't be talking in-depth about technical analysis. Nor will we discuss anything regarding all the other complexities that go into investing.

Having said that, you want to use this book to your advantage. Especially when you are more than likely a novice when it comes to investing. You might be wondering why you got interested in it in the first place.

Investing may seem like something that adults do. And there are many that do. The real question is: how many teenagers also invest in things such as the stock market or any kind of assets?

The answer just might surprise you. According to a 2022 study by Fidelity polling teens from 13 to 17, about one-fifth (or 20 percent) have started investing. Almost three-quarters of them admit that they have no prior knowledge of how to trade stocks or ETF/mutual funds.

Not only that, it may be a challenge for teenagers to find out where to begin with investing. This includes finding the right brokerage account. Or even educational information on how to invest as a teenager.

The good news is that you have this book as your starting point. You might have already researched on Google and found a whole slew of information. Some of it may give you this and others give you that.

Fortunately for you, this book will be able to provide you with all kinds of information on how you can invest your money. Thus, you are about to embark on an opportunity that may or may not be a once in a lifetime opportunity.

By once in a lifetime, we mean that you can only live through your teenage years once. For now, you are in the perfect time frame to invest and lay the groundwork for a prosperous financial future. Think about it: this puts you in an advantageous position compared to people older than you.

You can have a smile on your face knowing that you have all that time to learn about investing. Meanwhile, that time will allow you to ride out any market changes. The ups, downs, and topsy-turvey turns will certainly play a role in the returns you'll earn - be it short-term or long-term.

WHY INVEST AS A TEENAGER?

There may be plenty of reasons why you want to consider investing as a teenager. Let's take a look at what they are so you can be able to have a good idea for doing it on your own:

A CHANCE TO BUILD WEALTH

Simply put, investing can be a great tool for building wealth. Indeed, most adults that have invested have already experienced the highs and lows of the market. Including the declines and the bubbles that had burst.

Even thinking about them may make someone feel daunted by the stock market. But it has its own natural cycles that consist of crashes and growth periods. Historically, the market averages a yearly return of ten percent.

So that should give you a little bit of confidence. But think about it like this - a 46-year-old adult who started investing 30 years ago at 16 starting with $1000 will now have a portfolio worth $17500. That is not a typo.

This is what we mean when you are at one of the most advantageous moments in life. Compound interest is one of the best benefits to have starting out as a teenage investor. And you get to enjoy the fruits of that later on in life.

However, we're not telling you to invest $1000 and just let it sit there. The point of course is to grow wealth. Which means regularly contributing to those investments.

And the more that you contribute, the more you are able to see those returns. Imagine how much money you might have on hand when you reach your 30s, 40s, and so on. You may retire younger than the average person.

You might even use that money to build a business. It all depends on your financial goals - whatever those might be.

Financial independence

How can we blame anyone for wanting to be financially independent? Investing will allow you the chance to do so. And at the age that you are now, you have that breathing room.

Which means you can attain that goal even if you have dealt with your share of losses and gains. After all, no one has ever achieved success without going through the ups and downs of personal wealth building and financial independence.

Granted, you have a head start and plenty of time to ride out the waves. No matter how long they last, you can just say "surfs up" without any kind of worry at all. As long as you make regular contributions to your portfolio regardless of the market's direction, then you're going to see yourself sitting pretty on plenty of cold hard cash.

How much, you ask? It depends on your investment style, how much you contribute, and several other factors. Financial independence will give you plenty of freedom.

The freedom from debt that may tie you down. The ability to spend your money how you want, when you want, and where you want. And if you feel like it, it gives you a chance to earn and spend money without having to rely on a regular 9-to-5 job.

Again, financial independence also gives you leverage to start a business. The best part is that you may not have to rely on loans or raise more capital - even at the risk of being rejected by anyone who even gives you a few minutes to present your business idea.

Inflation

Inflation has been a hot topic for a long time - on and off. At the time of this writing, it's being discussed in the news. Prices increase every year, leading to the loss of value regarding your money.

On average, inflation is approximately three percent. This means that uninvested cash will lose three percent of its value each year. However, investing can lead to opportunities that will help protect your money from the grips of inflation.

Even better, there are some investment assets that will help you out as a hedge. This includes stocks, bonds, ETFs, mutual funds, even real estate. Now, before we say anything - we are not going to discuss how to invest in complex assets such as real estate.

For one, real estate investing is a ton of work. And it is something a teenager should not consider until they are older. Believe us, we have heard some stories about real estate investors dealing with property issues, bad tenants, and so on.

We may be digressing, but just a friendly reminder that we want to keep you away from the complex investments that are out there. Having said this, it is possible for you to hedge against inflation by way of investments.

WHAT WILL YOU LEARN IN THIS BOOK?

Of course, you will learn about investing in this book. However, it won't be the only thing that we will cover. Before you even consider investing, it's important to know some things about financial literacy.

With over 70 percent of teenagers not knowing how to trade stocks or ETFs, the question that needs to be asked is: how much do they know about financial literacy? Can they read bank statements?

Do they know the difference between income and expenses? This might be worrisome. However, you're going to learn the basics of financial literacy. The first two chapters will focus on that.

Speaking of chapters, let's provide you with an overview of what you will learn in this book:

- **Chapter 1: Introduction to investing:** This will discuss the importance of investing in a young age. You will also be introduced to how you can achieve long-term goals while learning how to build financial discipline. This will also introduce you to financial literacy and how it will work to your advantage. Finally, you will learn about the common misconceptions of investing and how to set financial goals that you can follow.

- **Chapter 2: Building a strong financial foundation:** You will learn one of the first steps towards investing. That is budgeting and saving. You'll also understand income and expenses and how you can become more financially literate. This also includes knowing how to build up an emergency fund so you can be financially prepared for the unexpected.

- **Chapter 3: Basic concepts of investing:** This will introduce you (for a bit) to stocks, bonds, and ETFs. You will also learn about the concept of risk and return. We'll discuss one of the most important concepts of investing known as diversification. By the time you finish reading this chapter, you will have a baseline of understanding on how investing works.

- **Chapter 4: Developing an investing strategy:** You'll learn about developing investment objectives and risk tolerances. This will also help you decide what kind of investor you plan on becoming. Do you plan on becoming conservative, aggressive, or balanced? We'll also delve into the long-term and short-term aspect of investing and discuss key terms that distinguish the two. And finally, you'll learn how to adopt the mindset of a young investor so you can be able to see the whole investing experience from a different angle compared to your peers.

- **Chapter 5: Stocks and Mutual Funds/ETFs - Everything you need to know:** This chapter will discuss everything you'll need to know about stocks, mutual funds, and ETFs. These are without question some of the best investment assets a young investor can start out with. You will learn how each of these work along with their pros and cons. We will also discuss the differences between stocks and mutual funds/ETFs.

- **Conclusion - Becoming a confident investor:** This will be the final chapter where we will wrap everything up. We'll recap everything that you have learned throughout the book. Along with it, we'll send you some words of encouragement along with tips for ongoing investment success. We believe that you have the ability to become a successful trader. And you have chosen the best time to get started. Passing up the opportunity may not be a good decision. Especially if you are serious about building your wealth.

A FEW MORE THINGS

Before we go any further, let's go over a few things. It's important that you pay close attention to this part since this will be an educational style book:

- This book does not guarantee quick gains. Nor is this a 'get rich quick book'. There are no guarantees when it comes to investing to begin with considering the amount of risks and rewards that exist.

- There are online brokers that won't allow anyone under the age of 18 to sign up for a trading account. However, to help you navigate through the challenge - we've included a bonus just for purchasing this book. It is a list of brokers that offer parent-teen custodial accounts for trading purposes along with other resources to check out for your investment education.

- We are not financial advisors. Nor should this book be mistaken for actual, professional financial advice. If you have any questions or concerns about all things financial - there are financial advisors that can help. They can be found locally or online - whichever you prefer.

WHAT'S NEXT?

There's only one thing left for you to do now. That is to buckle up - because you're in for a ride that we think that you are going to enjoy. There is nothing more exciting quite like the idea of learning how to invest so you can build a solid financial future.

This is your chance to learn more about it. This is a time to take advantage of that head start not many of your peers might have. So if you are interested in learning how to invest and be successful, turn the page and we'll begin with Chapter 1.

CHAPTER 1

Introduction to Investing

You decided to go forward to learning more about investing. Good choice. It's always a good idea to get a good introduction of what it is.

This chapter is intended for doing that. You will understand the importance of investing at a young age. We'll also talk about why financial literacy is important.

As a young person, you might be faced with many different opinions on investing. You may be easily persuaded to believe one opinion over the other. However, the thing to know is that there may be negative opinions on investing.

There are different misconceptions about it as well. We'll go over what those are in this chapter. Finally, you'll learn how you can set financial goals and be able to create a long-term vision for yourself.

This all-important chapter will lay one part of the foundation of investing. As someone who is in their teens, you are beginning at one of the best times of your life. People older than you are always wishing that they started something earlier in life.

With your whole life ahead of you (including adulthood), there's a lot you will learn about investing among all other things. If you are someone who wants to be serious about their money and their financial future - investing might be one of the best vehicles.

Let's dive right in to discuss more about investing and why it's important.

UNDERSTANDING THE IMPORTANCE OF INVESTING AT A YOUNG AGE

Investing at the age you are right now can have an incredible and profound impact on your financial future. There are plenty of advantages you'll experience as you are investing. Here are some points that you can consider while developing an understanding of how investments work and how it can help build your financial stability:

THE POWER OF COMPOUNDING

One of the most significant benefits of investing at a young age is the power of compounding. Compounding is defined as the ability of an investment to generate earnings. Over time, those earnings will earn their own.

In other words, those earnings snowball and get larger in number over time. When you start early, you're in an excellent position to enjoy those compounds that occur for many years over. Think about it - the exponential growth will increase over a long period of time.

Who knows? You may have enough to retire on before you're 50 years old. However, it depends on the source of income you have.

You could be working a regular job. Or you could go the self-employed route (which is easier today thanks to the Internet and the emergence of remote work). Either way, you will need a source of income to begin with.

You invest a specific amount over a period of time and watch it grow. That compounding interest and earnings will grow year-after-year, even if there are periods of sustained growth or some losses here and there.

TIME TO RECOVER FROM LOSSES

Of course, we can't say that investing comes with its share of risks. This includes taking on losses. When you are starting out at a young age, you have plenty of time to grow your wealth by way of investing.

At some point, you will experience losses. They can happen in the short-term. Here's the good news - you'll have more time to recover from these losses including the ones you experience from market downturns. As a young investor, you can afford to take on more risk.

The reason for this is that you will have a longer time horizon to ride out any fluctuations of the markets and be able to recover any losses in the process. Don't confuse this as a green light for taking intentionally risky investments.

Don't swing for the fences when it's OK to aim for a base hit. Or even line drive into the outfield for extra bases. Forgive us for the baseball references - but the point is that just because you can afford more risks, we're not saying you can afford to try and swing for the fences and go for the most volatile, high-risk and high-reward investments.

You basically have all kinds of room to take on losses that happen outside of your control such as market fluctuations. You can still recover the losses over an undetermined period of time. Yet, you have a greater time advantage compared to your older investor counterparts.

YOU LEARN TO BUILD FINANCIAL DISCIPLINE

At a young age, it is the perfect time to learn and develop financial discipline such as good money management habits. This includes but is not limited to setting aside a percentage of your income - which instills responsibility and planning for the future. This goes beyond investing and other positive impacts on your financial future.

Financial discipline pertains to doing your due diligence on something you want to invest in. Likewise, the same can be said about something you intend to purchase. In today's world, there are people who will look at customer reviews.

They can make a decision based on what people are saying about a certain product or service. If it sounds like a good investment that will help fulfill a specific need, then it must be worth spending. However, there's a fine line between essential spending and discretionary spending.

We'll discuss these two types of spending later on in the book. However, investing is part of the building blocks that consist of financial discipline. You'll determine whether or not a stock is a good investment for a certain reason (or why it's not for another).

LONG-TERM GOAL ACHIEVEMENTS

A young investor will have an early head start in achieving long-term financial success. This includes but not limited to paying for education, purchasing their first car or home, or even retiring comfortably. Starting early in life will give you plenty of opportunities to grow your investment rewards.

Needless to say, you will have all kinds of time to grow a large sum of money. This will also reduce any pressure of financial challenges that may occur in life. Plus, it also takes off any worry about having to save a lot of money when you are older.

They say 'time is money'. However, we say it in this context - the more time you have to work with, the more money you stand to gain. Whether it's through saving, investment, or both - these two elements can work in your favor.

IT PROVIDES YOU WITH PLENTY OF LEARNING OPPORTUNITIES

Investing at a young age allows you to to learn about different investment strategies, options, and how the financial markets function. This will give you an opportunity to understand the concepts of risk and return, diversification, asset allocation, and the importance of long-term investment approaches.

You'll gain plenty of knowledge and experience over the course of time. You'll also prove yourself to make informed financial decisions now and in the years that follow. It is important that you consider that you take as much time as you can to learn about investing with the help of a paper trading account.

If you are planning on trading stocks, there are plenty of apps and websites that will help you learn how to trade on the stock market. You won't be trading with real money - but you will be starting out with an account with a preset amount of 'money' (depending on the app you use).

There are different online stock trading websites that will offer paper trading accounts. Find one that will allow you to paper trade for free. It's always a good idea to find a place where you can educate yourself on the stock market and make trades at the same time.

Furthermore, it will give you a chance to get your feet wet and learn the ins and outs before you start investing with real money. You may have a strategy that you can try out for yourself. Give yourself a few months to paper trade before you make the decision to move forward with investing with actual money that you have.

In other words, don't rush into the whole thing. Don't spend a day paper trading and then jump into a real trading account the next. Give yourself time to learn stock investing.

Also, take advantage of any educational materials that are accessible to you (particularly for free).

FLEXIBILITY AND FREEDOM

As you start out early, you have more flexibility and greater room to achieve financial freedom. Your investment will grow and generate additional income. This will also give you the opportunity to pursue your much larger goals that may require money.

For example, if you plan on starting a business - you can have the capital on hand to lay the groundwork. You can invest in the equipment and other items you may need to operate. Not only that, you have plenty of breathing room in the event of emergencies or unexpected expenses.

OVERCOMING INFLATION

Inflation can take a bite out of the purchasing power of money over time. If you invest early, you will be able to outpace inflation and retain or grow the value of your wealth. Historically, investments have provided higher returns compared to a savings account - whether it's at a major or local bank.

Having investments will help you combat the impact of inflation. The more investments you have, the better prepared that you are.

THE IMPORTANCE OF FINANCIAL LITERACY

Financial literacy is important to have in today's world. It will help you make an informed decision related to your finances. There are reasons why you need to learn about it and understand the basics. Here's what they are:

PERSONAL FINANCIAL MANAGEMENT

With good financial literacy, you will be able to know how to manage your personal finances effectively. You will be able to learn the basics of budgeting, saving, and investing. This will ensure that your income is allocated properly and aligned with your own financial goals.

You'll also learn about making informed financial decisions regarding spending and debt management. All the while, you'll achieve more financial stability over time.

AVOIDING DEBT AND MANAGING CREDIT

Your credit will be just as important as the rest of your financial standing. The better your credit, the better your chances of being approved for loans will increase. Not only that, you will need to learn about interest rates, credit scores, and debt management.

This will ensure that you won't take on excessive debt. Meanwhile, it will also help you learn about responsible borrowing decisions. A financially literate person will know the difference between good debt and bad debt. They'll also learn about how they can make payments on time and avoid any financial traps that may lead to financial struggles that can last years.

MAKING OTHER INFORMED INVESTMENT DECISIONS

Every informed financial decision will be tied to your financial literacy levels. The stronger you are in financial literacy, the better chance you'll make the right decision - albeit strategically. You'll be thinking about your current financial situation.

This includes how much money you have in the bank, your potential returns, the level of risk in the investment, and whether or not these align with your risk tolerance or financial goals. Likewise, it is important to consider what is essential spending and what is discretionary.

As promised, let's inform you on the difference between the two:

Essential spending: This consists of household expenses including groceries, utilities, mortgage/rent, and other expenses that are considered essential. These will pertain to the things you'll need on a regular basis. Including the basic human needs of food and shelter among others.

Discretionary spending: This is your optional spending. For example, discretionary spending includes items such as video games, streaming services, additional clothing, and other non-essential items and expenses. You'll have the option to determine whether or not spending on such things can provide you a positive return on investment.

In other words, if you spend money on a non-essential item, how do you know if it was money worth spending? If it satisfies a need, then you know that it's a positive return on the money you've spent on it. Sometimes, a return on "investment" isn't always money.

It's the happiness and satisfaction of what you spent it on. Now, we talk about investment in the context of spending money on an item. So it's not to be confused with the kind of investments we'll be talking about throughout the remainder of the book.

PLANNING FOR RETIREMENT

You're probably thinking that it's way too early to think about retirement. But being financially literate will be key to helping you plan for it as you get older. You'll be able to understand the different types of retirement accounts that exist like IRAs, 401ks, and so on.

You'll learn about how they work, how you can contribute, and how you can build it up with the help of the investments you make in the future. You can be able to estimate your retirement needs along with your net savings goals, and make the best investment choices possible to ensure that your financial future is secure.

ENTREPRENEURSHIP AND BUSINESS MANAGEMENT

If you are planning on starting and managing a business, being financially literate is a must. It will help you understand financial statements, cash flow management, profit margins, and plenty of various business figures. You'll be able to read the pertinent documents that pertain to running a business.

This way, you can be able to make informed decisions based on what's in front of you for proper documentation. At the same time, it will help you secure more financing for your business. It can also be helpful in negotiating contracts with vendors, and understanding the tax implications tied to a business that you run (assuming you qualify).

CONSUMER AWARENESS AND PROTECTION

Financial literacy protects you from making poor financial decisions. Especially the ones that may feel like it's in good faith - but turns out not being the case. In other words, you may be spending money and you may have been a victim of fraudulent scams, predatory practices, and other similar situations.

It is important to compare financial products and services. This also means doing your due diligence. That alone doesn't apply to just investing in stocks or any other assets being traded on the market. It pertains to what you intend to purchase - be it a one-time purchase, a recurring payment, or something else.

It is important that you also read the terms and conditions (if and when applicable). Yes, it may contain legal language that may be hard to understand. So if you're in doubt, the best option is not to go forward with it.

It's also a good idea to identify the signs of a possible scam. As a teenager, you need to be aware of these as soon as possible. Not everything is always the real thing.

Scams can affect anyone. The most vulnerable are usually younger people like yourself and even senior citizens. But you can be more informed by learning the following signs and red flags that pertain to scams or fraudulent information, they include but are not limited to the following:

- **An issue or a prize that is involved:** If you get a notification that you won a lottery or contest and are told to claim a prize, it's best to ignore it. Especially if you never entered a contest in the first place. If you enter your name, that's one thing (assuming it's legitimate). But even if it looks real, you need to look closely at any details. If anything seems amiss, then don't go forward with it.

- **You are confronted with an urgent demand:** A scammer may often pressure someone to take a specific action fast or make a quick decision. It may be enough to make a poor decision. That is why it is important to consider doing your research before you do anything else.

- **Unexpected charges appear on your bank account:** If someone has unauthorized access to your bank account, they may have your debit or credit card information. From there, they'll make purchases that you didn't actually make yourself.

- **You receive an unexpected check or credit card:** A check may arrive by mail or other delivery methods like UPS. It may require a signature and no further instructions. The same applies to credit cards. Whatever you do, do not sign the document. Nor should you receive or cash the check. The same applies for credit cards you didn't apply for - don't use it.

- **You are threatened with severe consequences if you don't comply:** Using the unexpected check example, there may be a threat of imprisonment if you don't cash it. There may be other scams done over the phone that may threaten the same thing about taxes or other financial situations. This has been a common type of fraud that has targeted all kinds of people in recent years.

- **It seems too good to be true:** One of the more self-explanatory signs of a scam. If it sounds too good to be true, it's more than likely that it is.

- **You are asked to pay for something ahead of time:** You may be asked to pay using cryptocurrency, money wires, gift cards, or some unusual form of payment. This is a red flag that many people are picking up on. You may be asked to use this form of payment in advance in exchange for something that may be promised to you. Avoid this at all costs.

Hopefully at this point, you've gained some kind of financial literacy that can save you money. And yes, even frustration and legal headaches. It is important that you avoid scams at all costs. The more you know about the signs, the better you will be able to spot them.

ECONOMIC STABILITY AND WELL-BEING

A financially literate person will contribute to their economy and their overall well-being. When this happens, they are less likely to face financial distress and rely on social safety nets - including those provided by the government. This can be due to the face that a person can make sound financial decisions.

All while contributing to the economy by way of savings and investment. As a result, they will have greater confidence and control over their own financial lives.

THE COMMON MISCONCEPTIONS OF INVESTING DEBUNKED

Of course, you're going to hear a ton of different sentiments about investing. Including a handful of these common misconceptions that get thrown around. If you have even dabbled in a bit of research regarding investing, you've probably heard of them by now.

Let's take a look at what they are and why they aren't the kind of points you want to take to heart:

INVESTING IS ONLY FOR THE WEALTHY

This is one of the most prevalent misconceptions out there. The reality is that anyone with a small amount of money can start investing. You'll have a good number of investment options - even if your level of income happens to be lower than someone else's.

For example, you can take advantage of fractional shares or low-cost index funds. Remember, starting early will give you the advantage to grow your wealth over time. That way, you'll have more breathing room in terms of the assets you can invest in.

One thing to be aware of is that there are stock accounts that require a small to no minimum deposit. This may be a thing to search for when it comes time to choose one that will work best for your investing and financial goals.

INVESTING IS EQUAL TO GAMBLING

This is still a misconception, even though there are some people who would "gamble" everything on a stock or asset, hoping for a large gain. And yet, they lose it all without having to perform the standard operating procedures of investing including due diligence or even have a shred of understanding of how the stock market works.

However, in this context - this assumes that you need luck to succeed in the stock market due to uncertain outcomes. Yes, there is an element of risk involved. For that reason, it is important to follow a standard procedure that we believe is required for a smart investor to do.

This includes analysis, research, and diversifying your asset portfolio. Doing this not only mitigates risks, but it also increases the likelihood of getting positive returns. Compare that to actual gambling, which relies primarily on chance and has no underlying value or analysis.

People can argue about gambling terms, theory, and "analysis" all they want. But gambling and investing are not the same.

TIMING IS ESSENTIAL FOR SUCCESS

Many individuals will believe that you can succeed in the stock market if you time it just right. Yet, here's the issue: the timing is extremely difficult - even for professionals who have traded for years. Trying to time the market leads to missed opportunities and potential losses.

Instead of worrying about timing, you want to focus on a long-term investment strategy that stays true to your financial goals. At the same time, it would be best to stay invested through the market fluctuations.

However, there's a good time to buy a stock and a bad time. Again, this can be decided based on the analysis and research that you do. Once you get into the more intermediate and advanced details of due diligence, you may find that there may be a stock that isn't worth buying at the right time for whatever reason.

It can be due to the fact that the company may not be performing well (and the numbers won't lie). Instead, focus on the long-term investing strategies and you'll worry less about timing.

If you find out about a missed opportunity, don't worry about it. They happen. Every successful investor in the world has experienced them multiple times.

INVESTING REQUIRES EXTENSIVE KNOWLEDGE

This is a misconception that can be tricky to understand. While it's a plus to have good financial literacy, a better understanding of different stock market terms and statistics, and similar items - you don't need to possess a lot of financial knowledge or become an expert.

Financial literacy is not a prerequisite for investing, despite a valuable skill to have. It's also important to note that there are experts out there such as financial advisors that will deal with the difficult things so you won't have to. Plus, online investing platforms will have plenty of educational materials that will help you navigate the investment landscape and make informed decisions.

INVESTMENT IS FOR OLDER INDIVIDUALS

This is not quite the misconception you want to listen to. Otherwise, you will be robbed of that time advantage that we've discussed throughout the book so far. A young investor will have plenty of time to grow their wealth compared to their older counterparts.

The sooner you start, the better. And it will better your chances of building a strong financial future.

HIGH RETURNS ARE GUARANTEED

This is where a lot of people will go into investing for the wrong reasons. They expect high returns - albeit on a guaranteed basis. Yes, while investing has the potential to provide you with substantial returns, they happen over a long-term basis.

To further debunk this misconception, we have to mention that market fluctuations, economic conditions, and individual investment choices all play a role in the amount of returns you get. As always, you will need to diversify your investments, have a long-term perspective, and understand that returns can vary.

INVESTING IS A ONE-TIME DECISION

Needless to say, investing is not some one-time decision that doesn't require ongoing monitoring and adjustments. In order to be a successful investor, you will need to monitor your assets while having a willingness to reassess your strategies and rebalance your portfolios.

Market conditions, personal circumstances, and your financial goals can change over time. For those reasons, adjusting your investment plans may be necessary. Keep that in mind while you are looking at your portfolio and adding on other assets over a period of time.

SETTING FINANCIAL GOALS AND CREATING A LONG-TERM VISION AS A TEENAGER

It's always a good idea to consider setting financial goals and a long-term vision. At your age, it's a wise and proactive approach towards building a future that is secure and prosperous. Here are some of the things you'll want to consider in order to establish your financial goals and develop a long-term vision:

REFLECT ON YOUR VALUES AND ASPIRATIONS

Spend time on reflecting your values, aspirations, and what you want to achieve in your life. Consider your passions, interests, and the kind of lifestyle that you envision for yourself. You also want to understand your values and aspirations will help you align your financial goals with your other life goals - small or large.

DEFINE YOUR SPECIFIC AND MEASURABLE GOALS

It's always a good idea to set specific and measurable financial goals that are aligned with your long-term vision. This may include saving a specific amount of money for college, starting a business, traveling, or purchasing a home. You want to make your goals clear and definitive so you can be able to track your progress and make the necessary adjustments along the way.

Don't be too vague in your definitions. And at the same time, try not to be hyper specific. Just be as clear and definitive as possible and make adjustments if there happens to be certain changes that occur both in your investment portfolio - and outside of it.

PRIORITIZE YOUR GOALS

There are some financial goals that need to go ahead of others. This will be due to their importance and feasibility. Not to mention, some of these financial goals will need to require more immediate attention.

Goals like saving up for education may be more of a priority compared to long-term objectives such as retirement. When you prioritize your goals, it helps you allocate your resources effectively while keeping focused on what matters most to you.

BREAK DOWN YOUR GOALS INTO ACTIONABLE STEPS

Your goals can be broken down into smaller, actionable steps. This can make them more manageable while giving you a clear roadmap for achieving them. To give you an example, you can set a monthly savings target and identify the expenses to reduce or eliminate so you can accelerate your savings.

Once again, adjustments may be necessary while you are en route to your goals. Especially if there are instances that happen beyond your control such as unexpected expenses. But nevertheless, if you can break down your goals into actionable steps that are easy to take - you should be in good shape now and in the long-term.

DEVELOP GOOD SAVING AND BUDGETING HABITS

Cultivating the habit of saving and budgeting is key. Especially when it's earlier on in life. As a teenager, now is the perfect time to learn about it.

Start creating a budget that will allow you to track your income and expenses. Also, aim to save a portion of your income on a regular basis. If possible, automate your savings.

Building a strong saving and budgeting habit will keep you ahead of the curve. Plus, it'll help you achieve your financial goals while solidifying your financial security.

LEARN ABOUT PERSONAL FINANCES ON YOUR OWN

Self-education is so important when it comes to valuable skills. You can learn so much from those that know it well like your parents, teachers, and others. However, part of knowing something requires learning it on your own at times.

It's also a good idea to read books, attend workshops, and even check out any reliable online resources that may exist. If you need to, seek out the help of professional financial experts or mentors. At a young age, being able to build financial literacy can help you build the skills and knowledge that will come in handy for when it comes time to make informed decisions on your financial future while navigating the complex nature of personal finances (including investing).

STAY FOCUSED AND FLEXIBLE

The important thing to remember is that your long-term vision and financial goals are your primary focus. However, you need to be willing to be adaptable due to circumstances that can change. Life can present to you plenty of opportunities and challenges - albeit unexpectedly.

You will need to be flexible and adjust your plans accordingly. This is why you need to regularly reassess your goals, monitor your progress, and make necessary adjustments if something were to arise.

When setting financial goals and creating a long-term vision at your age, you're putting yourself ahead of your peers. You might even be leading by example to help them do the same thing.

BOTTOM LINE

While investing can be a challenge, understanding it will give you a clear idea of how it all works. You know about the kind of benefits it will give you while being able to know the risks. You may have a certain financial goal that may be met thanks to investing.

It is important that you learn about the ins and outs of investing and even personal finances as a whole. The good news - you don't need to spend every waking hour knowing everything about it. When the time comes, you will need to practice investing with the help of a paper trading account.

You don't need to be a financial genius to be a successful investor. As long as you adopt the right mindset and have clear goals - it will be easier for you to succeed at investing compared to someone who won't because of the reckless decisions they've made.

Also, steer clear of any of the misconceptions that we've mentioned earlier in this chapter. Investing even as a teenager is a bit easier. Especially when there are plenty of barriers that have since been removed. For example, those barriers include high minimum deposits for investing and even the lack of accessibility of trading platforms.

Thanks to the Internet and smartphones, accessing online trading platforms is easier than ever. But let's not dive too far into them just yet. We still have a bit more ground to cover.

CHAPTER 2

Building a Strong Financial Foundation

Before we get into the heart of investing, we need to discuss the importance of building a strong financial foundation. This will play a huge role in your investing journey. In the previous chapter, we've discussed how challenges and circumstances can play a role in your financial futures and the goals you intend to achieve.

Thus, you want to make sure that you're able to build a financial foundation that is strong enough to handle any necessary changes. Setbacks can happen. Unexpected events beyond your control may pop up any time and any place.

It can require money to solve the issue. But it can set you back a bit in terms of meeting your financial goals. Do you have the financial foundation to handle these setbacks and market fluctuations (among others)?

If not, don't worry. This chapter will show you how to get it done. You will learn how to budget and save, which will be a crucial element towards investing.

We'll teach you how to understand income and expenses. This way, you'll be able to easily navigate through a personal budget (and maybe other financial statements for when you decide to start a business). Finally, we'll discuss how you can create an emergency fund so you can be prepared to handle any unexpected expenses should any arise.

By the end of this chapter, you'll have a base level of financial literacy to work with. And that may be enough for the purpose of investing. Yet, it never hurts to go a little further with it if you feel that is the case.

Let's begin now with how you can build a strong financial foundation as soon as today.

BUDGETING AND SAVING: THE FIRST STEPS TOWARDS INVESTING

One of the first crucial steps towards successful investing is budgeting and saving. You are laying the foundation for financial stability and providing the necessary funds to start building your wealth.

Budgeting is the process of creating a plan that allows you to allocate your income and expenses. You will be tracking these major elements on a regular basis. While you do this, you will need to identify your financial goals and make them as clear as possible.

You should determine how much you can afford to spend on various categories. As a teenager, you won't have to worry about expenses such as mortgage/rent or any expenses pertaining to what your parents are spending. However, there may be an arrangement made by you and your parents where you are chipping in for the essential expenses they need to pay.

Otherwise, it is important to take a look at what your essential expenses are. You may have a car, so your expenses may be for gas, maintenance, or even paying your part of the insurance (if you are covered under your parents' car insurance policy). Your essential expenses will likely differ compared to what your parents are facing.

There are still other expenses to keep an eye on including food, entertainment, and savings. Again, pay attention to both your essential and discretionary spending. It's better to keep your discretionary spending to a minimum, if possible.

A well-designed budget will help you gain a clear understanding of your cash flow. All while you make informed decisions on how you spend that money.

Let's take a look at more reasons why budgeting and saving should be important for investment purposes:

EXPENSE CONTROL

Budgeting allows you to have control over your expenses. It will allow you to prioritize your spending and cut back on unnecessary or impulsive purchases. You'll create a surplus of funds that are created by way of this method of expense control - which is directed towards saving and investments.

SAVING FOR EMERGENCIES

Building an emergency fund is another crucial step to take. We'll go into more detail about this later on in the chapter. But for now, let's say this should be a part of your budget that you should never skip (or skimp on) and for good reason.

CAPITAL FOR INVESTMENTS

Of course, there's going to be the need for capital when it comes time to invest. When you save money, it will help you build up the amount you need to get started. The real question is: what assets are you intent on investing?

The important thing to remember is that the more capital you have, the more flexible you'll be on your investments. As we've mentioned earlier, the barriers of capital requirements have lowered compared to ages past.
Meaning that there are little to no minimum deposits needed for investing - depending on the platform you go with. Yes, there are still some minimums out there that may require hundreds or even thousands of dollars.

But as a teenager, it may be a good idea to start out with a minimum deposit that best suits your financial goals and how much you are willing to invest initially.

THE OPPORTUNITY TO DEFINE YOUR INVESTMENT GOALS

This would be a good time to determine what you want to achieve with your investments. Is it a down payment for a home? A college education? Or is it something else?

Remember, you need to make the goal as clear and definitive as possible. This way, you'll want to be able to align your investment strategy accordingly. You have plenty of time to create a positive return on investments despite the market fluctuations and other activities that may cause your investments to go up, down, or even sideways.

A CHANCE TO LEARN ABOUT DIFFERENT INVESTMENTS

This might also be a good time to learn about the different investment assets that exist. These include stocks, bonds, mutual funds, ETFs, and other assets. They say knowledge is power - and that tends to be true.

You'll have the power to know about the kind of assets that you can invest in. This includes the advantages and disadvantages of each one. Especially the ones that pertain to whether or not they can help you meet your financial goals on a long-term basis.

START WITH THE LOW-RISK OPTIONS

Granted, the low-risk options should be something a beginner investor should focus on. As a teenager, this should be your best starting point. This will familiarize you with how low-risk investments like index funds, ETFs, and even bank CDs work.

One of the main reasons why these options are great are because they have lower fees. Meaning they won't take a bite into your savings. At the same time, these options will be beneficial in terms of your long-term investment goals.

PORTFOLIO DIVERSIFICATION

We'll hammer this point home for as many times as we need to. Diversification in investment is a super important part of the whole entire process. You should be spreading your portfolio across different assets.
If you're going to stick with stocks, don't invest in one industry or sector. You'll want to diversify to different industries as you go. You can also diversify your investments across different asset classes, geographical regions, or sectors.

If and when you diversify, you'll be able to reduce the impact of any single investment performance on your overall portfolio. In other words, if a stock falls, it won't drag down the rest of your portfolio.

This is why the term "never put your eggs in one basket" exists. And for the best reasons.

REGULAR REVIEW AND ADJUSTMENT

Periodically, you want to review your investments to ensure that they align with your goals and risk tolerance. Your financial situation may change. If they do, you'll want to adjust your investment strategy accordingly.

In the meantime, you will need to keep yourself informed of the market trends. If you need professional advice, don't be afraid to reach out. Whether you are starting out as a teenager or a seasoned investor by the time you're 25 - there's no shame in seeking professional help whenever you are trying to figure out where to go in terms of your investment decisions and strategy.

But nevertheless, be ready to make adjustments if and when necessary. It can make the difference between maintaining your finances or losing out on potential gains.

INCOME AND EXPENSES EXPLAINED

Let's discuss income and expenses in simple terms:

- **Income:** This is the money you earn. There are different sources of income that exist. They include but are not limited to allowance from your parents, a part-time job, any odd jobs you do around the neighborhood, and others. This is the money that goes into your pocket.

- **Expenses:** In plain English, these are the items and services you spend money on. For example, buying clothes is an expense. You pay for expenses when hanging out with friends. In other words, expenses are where your money goes.

Now that you know the plain English definitions, you want to make sure you have good balance. Which means your expenses should not outweigh your income. Otherwise, you'll be "drowning in the red" as they say in business.

As a rule: don't spend more money than you actually have. This can lead to financial trouble later on in life. In order to help you prevent this, here are some tips on managing your income and expenses:

KEEP TRACK OF YOUR INCOME

Whatever money you earn, document it. It doesn't matter if it's your allowance, birthday money from Grandma, a part-time job, or whatever else. You should have a notebook handy to write down how much money you've earned and through a source of income.

If needed, include additional paperwork such as check stubs. Put them in an organized filing cabinet or folder. This way, you'll have the proper documentation confirming how you received the income.

Also, it may help to keep track of any income - especially later on in life when you may need to report it for tax purposes or appropriate situations.

ALSO TRACK YOUR EXPENSES

Tracking your expenses will also be key as well. Like your income, you will need to document what you spend money on as well. This will help you stay informed of where your money is going.

It will also help you make crucial financial decisions later on. You may find out whether or not you are spending too much on a certain thing. It may be easier to cut out those discretionary expenses if they are somehow getting in the way of your financial goals.

As such, being vigilant about tracking your income and expenses will be key. Especially when you need to know where your money is coming from (and where it goes on a regular basis). This kind of information will prove itself useful when it comes time to sit down and make potential adjustments to your budget.

SET FINANCIAL GOALS

Your financial goals should always be at the front of your mind. Especially when you are handling your money. Think about what they are regularly.

You may be considering the idea of spending money on something. The real question you want to ask yourself is: is now a good time to spend money on this product or that service? If so, why?

Think about what you are really saving up for. Is it something you really want? Is it something that you plan on doing in the next few years or so?

Remember, your financial goals are a priority. And needlessly spending money on things that don't really matter can set them back. The more you spend, the farther back you'll be away from your financial goals.

BE MINDFUL OF YOUR SPENDING

We've briefly touched on this in the previous example. It's important to ask yourself if spending money on a certain item or service is necessary. Yes, it's fine to treat yourself once in a while.

At the same time, you want to avoid overspending. This can jeopardize your financial well-being, even for the long-term. You may be saying, 'it's my money - I'll spend it on whatever I want'.

Be that as it may - but it's important to have a good financial future ahead of you. Because it can certainly give you plenty of advantages. Especially when you are navigating through certain complicated procedures that may require money like purchasing a house, a vehicle, or something else.

Plus, you can live a life free from any worry regarding bad debt. Your financial goals should always come first. So be mindful of your spending and your future self will thank you.

SET UP A BUDGET

Budgeting your money includes a list of income sources and your expenses. Also, be sure to set up a section where you are allocating your savings. This will help you plan how much money you can spend without going overboard.

THE IMPORTANCE OF AN EMERGENCY FUND AND HOW TO BUILD ONE FROM SCRATCH

An emergency fund is something that you need to set aside specifically for any emergencies or unexpected expenses. It is a safety net to protect you financially when unforeseen circumstances arise. They can happen at any time or any place.

There are certain circumstances that can be preventable depending on what they are. For example, checking your vehicle and maintaining it once in a while can prevent the unexpected expense of having to take it to an auto shop for emergency repairs. Others may occur beyond your control with little to no warning.

Regardless, it is important to be prepared when the unexpected hits you. Because you won't know for sure how much it will cost. You'll feel better knowing you'll have that amount to pay it off without having to dip into your savings.

With that in mind, let's take a look at the following tips on how you can build an emergency fund from scratch:

- **Set aside a certain percentage:** It's important to set aside a percentage of your income for total savings. For emergency expenses, a smart rule would be to set aside a total of 15 percent. 10 percent will be for the emergency fund while the other is for other savings. The reason why the emergency fund savings has a large percentage is that emergency expenses can be a bit costly. So the more money you tuck away for that purpose, the better prepared you'll be financially for any emergencies and unexpected expenses to pop up.

- **Start with an initial amount:** To set up an emergency fund, the money needs to be set aside in a savings account separate from other bank accounts you may have. As for an initial amount, you can decide how much money to put in to start out. This can be as low as $25. You can start off with a higher amount like $50 or $100 if you so choose. The more, the better.

- **Know how much is necessary:** A major rule of thumb for an emergency fund is keeping at least anywhere from three months to a year's worth of expenses in the account. The longer the protection period, the more security you will have. The amount of expenses between those time periods will always vary based on how much you spend on expenses every month. If you keep track of your expenses, crunch the numbers on how much you've spent in the previous month. Then multiply that by a specific number (like three). For example, let's say you spent $500 this past month on expenses. Three months of those expenses is $1500.

- **Remember why it's there:** You want to remember why the emergency fund exists. It's quite self-explanatory. It will also help you determine which account to use whenever you need access to cash. So if there are non-emergency expenses, leave the emergency fund alone and use the applicable account.

- **Automate, if possible:** We live in an age where automation is possible. Putting a percentage of money into an account can be tedious. Doing this with multiple accounts can be confusing. So it may be a good idea to automate your money and where it goes. For example, if you are receiving a regular income from a job, you'll need to set up automation where a certain amount of income will go towards one account, and another part goes to other applicable accounts such as your general savings. Once its taken care of, you won't have to worry about forgetting about putting money away. Or even putting it in the wrong account. This way, it prevents shortchanging your emergency fund.

Building an emergency fund takes time and commitment. It's OK to start out small. However, consistently building it up will be key.

It helps to keep focused on your savings goals. But saving up for emergency funds will be the most important. Even if you are also building up another account for general savings.

It may seem like you are juggling too many items. But with the help of automation - this will save you time and frustration. When the time comes for unexpected emergencies and events (and they do happen), you'll breathe a sigh of relief knowing that you are financially prepared.

Instead of feeling the sticker shock of an emergency expense, you'll say to yourself "no problem, I got the money to pay for it". Imagine staying calm and cool when emergency expenses arise. Compare that to facing that same situation and having little to no money to make the payment.

BOTTOM LINE

If you are serious about investing, the best thing to do going forward is having a stable financial foundation. This includes being able to budget and save your money. Building savings and having an emergency fund are solid pillars that will ensure that you can have enough cushion for investing your money.

Your financial goals are important. And budgeting and saving is all part of the plan. As is investing.

Think about it - when you do this, you might have enough capital for when it comes time to start off with investments. Be sure to keep your income and expenses balanced. Don't spend more money than you earn or you'll be setting yourself far back from the financial goals you've set to achieve.

CHAPTER 3

Basic Concepts of Investing

Now, we'll get more into the investing aspect of this book. What better way to kick it off with a chapter explaining the basic concepts. The chapter will introduce us to stocks, bonds, and mutual funds/ETFs.

In a later chapter, we'll describe these specific assets in more detail. Specifically, we'll discuss stocks and mutual funds and ETFs including how they all differ from one another. But we will provide you with some introductory details so you have a good idea of what we'll be discussing in the future.

We'll also talk about the concepts of risks and return. These are indeed two of the elements that make investing what it is. You can have good returns over a sustained period of time - but there are risks that will exist.

There are risks that will occur beyond your own control. However, mitigating them will be important. That is why we will be discussing diversification and asset allocation in this chapter as well.

By the end of this chapter, you will have a baseline understanding of investing and how it works. It will also set the stage on how you can learn how different investment assets function. So let's get right down to the nitty gritty here.

We hope you are excited to learn about the basic concepts of investing. Here we go.

STOCKS, BONDS, AND ETFs EXPLAINED

There are so many different assets that pertain to investing. We'll be introducing three of them in this chapter - stocks, bonds, and ETFs. Yes, there are different ones that we'll discuss later on including real estate (including REITs).

Let's define and explain each of these for a moment:

STOCKS

Stocks are one of the more common assets for beginner investors. These are known as shares or equities. A stock represents ownership in a publicly-traded company.

These have the potential to help generate profit based on the success of the company. They issue a stock as a means to raise capital for their operations and their growth. A stockholder will have voting rights that can play a role in a company's major decisions.

These include but are not limited to the appointment of the board of directors. Stock prices can fluctuate based on several different factors. They include but are not limited to company performance, industry trend, economic conditions, and investor sentiments among others.

BONDS

Bonds are debt instruments that are issued by governments, municipalities, and corporations. Like stocks, they are intended to be used to raise capital. An investor will purchase a bond - which essentially lends money to the issuer in exchange for regular interest payments (or coupon payments). This also includes the return of the principal amount at maturity.

Bonds are considered to be a more conservative investment compared to stocks. The reason for this is that they offer a fixed income and have a predetermined maturity date. Interest bonds can vary depending on several factors - including creditworthiness, prevailing market rates, and the term on the bond.

MUTUAL FUNDS

Mutual funds are investments where multiple investors will pool money to invest in a diversified portfolio of securities. They can include stocks, bonds, and other assets. These funds will be handled by professional fund managers.

They will make the investment decisions on behalf of the investors. Thus, this can be one of the more appealing options for teenagers starting out with stock investing. When you invest in these mutual funds, you are buying shares or units of the fund.

The value of these shares are known as net asset value or NAV. The NAV fluctuates based on the performance of the underlying investments. Mutual funds will offer investors the opportunity to invest in a diversified portfolio with relatively lower investment amounts and benefit from the management of professionals.

EXCHANGE-TRADED FUNDS (ETFs)

Exchange-traded funds or ETFs are investment funds that trade on stock exchanges in a similar manner to individual stocks. They are designed to track the performance of a specific index, sector, commodity, or asset class. ETFs hold a basket of underlying securities - again like stocks, bonds, or commodities.

They aim to replicate the investment returns of the chosen index or asset. ETFs will offer investors the ability to gain exposure to a wide range of assets or markets. Meanwhile, this is a cost-effective and easily tradable method of investing. These are bought or sold throughout the trading day at market prices.

One of the major differences it has with mutual funds is the latter has prices that are determined at the end of the day. In the chapter dedicated to ETFs and mutual funds, we'll discuss some of the other differences that they have.

RISK AND RETURN EXPLAINED

As mentioned, risk and return are paramount for investments. Without them, what would be the point? They are two fundamental concepts that are intertwined with one another.

Let's explain each of them in the following details:

RISK

Risk is defined as the potential for loss or uncertainty associated with an investment. It is a part of investing that is inherent as there is always a chance that an investment may not perform as expected. Therefore, it may result in a loss of capital.

There are two types of risk that exist in investing: systematic and unsystematic. Let's explain each of these right now:

- **Systematic risk:** This is the risk that affects the overall market or economy. Other factors that play a role include but are not limited to: economic conditions, political events, interest rates, and market volatility. These cannot be diversified away and can lead to sustained losses if such a situation is bad enough. All investments can be exposed to this kind of risk to some extent.

- **Unsystematic risk:** This is better known by the alternative terms of specific or diversifiable risk. This pertains to an individual investment or industry. This kind of risk can be reduced by way of diversification. The examples of unsystematic risk include but are not limited to: company-specific factors, industry trends, regulatory changes, or management decisions.

Investors must assess their risk tolerance while considering their financial goals and investment horizon while making investment decisions. As we've mentioned before, higher-risk investments do offer the potential for higher returns.

However, these can also carry a greater chance of loss. As a teenage investor, it is important to start off with a low-risk asset for investments starting out. Which means mutual funds and ETFs may be the best possible route to take.

RETURN

Returns are defined as the gain or loss that is generated from an investment over a specific period. It is expressed as a percentage or monetary amount. There are two main sources where a return can come from:

- **Capital appreciation:** This is the increase in value of an investment over time. One example of this is when you purchase a stock at $100 and then sell it at $150. This $50 increase represents capital appreciation. If there is a loss of $50, this is known as capital depreciation.

- **Income:** You can generate income by way of your investments. These can come in the form of dividends through stocks (if offered), interest via bonds, or rental payments (if you are investing real estate, which isn't suitable for teenagers. We'll explain why in a later chapter)

The relationship between risk and return is generally characterized by the principle of higher risk being associated with the potential for higher returns. Riskier investments like stocks or emerging market investments will tend to have the potential for higher returns.

This is compared to safer investments such as bonds or cash equivalents. The relationship between risk and return is not always guaranteed. As we've said before, higher returns also come with a higher chance of loss - and also a higher level of volatility.

A great loss can happen just as quickly as a great gain. If you are starting out as a teenage investor, it may not be a good idea to delve into the volatile or even most complex investment assets at the moment. Later on in the book, we'll explain why.

With that said, investors need to carefully evaluate the trade-off of risk and return based on their own individual circumstances and investment goals. Also, diversification, asset allocation, and risk management strategies can help balance the risk and return of a portfolio.

DIVERSIFICATION AND ASSET ALLOCATION

These two key principles of investment portfolio management are designed to mitigate risk while optimizing return. Let's explain diversification and asset allocation further:

DIVERSIFICATION

Diversification is a practice where you are spreading investments across different assets or classes in order to reduce risk. The idea behind this is that investing in a variety of assets that perform differently in different market conditions. For example, a poor performance in one investment can be offset by the positive performance of another.

Diversification can be achieved in three different ways:

- **Asset class diversification:** Allocating investments across different asset classes include stocks, bonds, real estate, commodities, and cash. Each of these classes behave differently in response to economic conditions. Thus, diversifying can help reduce the impact of one class's poor performance by investing in others that would perform well in the same situation. This can soften the blow of impact for your profile as a whole. One good reason why the 'eggs in one basket' strategy is the worst thing ever.

- **Sector/Industry Diversification:** Within each asset class, you can diversify investments across different sectors in industries. For example, let's take a look at stocks. You can reduce your risk by investing in different industries. So instead of investing in technology stocks, consider diversifying by investing in the energy or travel industry. If an industry takes a hit and your portfolio consists of nothing but those kinds of stocks, you're in for a rough time.

- **Geographic diversification:** This pertains to investing in different geographic regions or countries to reduce exposure to country-specific risks. These include economic, political, and regulatory events that may be affected by the country in particular. It can have a lesser impact if you are diversifying your portfolio based on geography.

Keep in mind that diversification can be useful in terms of mitigating unsystematic risk. However, it won't be able to eliminate any systematic risks that may threaten your portfolio. Plus, diversification does not guarantee profits.

Simply put, it can reduce the overall volatility and risk associated with the portfolio as a whole.

ASSET ALLOCATION

Asset allocation involves determining the optimal distribution of investments across different asset classes based on an investor's financial goals, risk tolerance, and investment time horizon. This strategic decision of how much of the portfolio's total value should be allocated to various asset classes.

We've already mentioned that stocks and bonds are main asset classes. Cash and other alternative investments are among the others. The goal of asset allocation is to create a portfolio that is balanced while aligned with the investor's risk-return objectives.

Asset allocation decisions are based on the principle that different asset classes have varying levels of risk and return potential. In one example, let's take a look at stocks. Stocks are considered higher risk but with a potential for higher returns over the long-term.
Bonds are lower risk and thus offer lower potential returns. The asset allocation decision can be influenced by several different factors. One of them includes the investor's time horizon (short-term or long-term).

Other factors include risk tolerance, investment objectives, and market conditions. You want to periodically review and rebalance the asset allocation as the market conditions and investor's goals can change over time.

When diversifying across different asset classes and strategically allocating investments, investors aim to create a well-balanced portfolio that seeks to optimize returns while managing risks according to their own objectives and individual circumstances.

BOTTOM LINE

These basic concepts should give you a good idea of the kind of assets that exist. You know the differences between them and how they operate. Now, you have an understanding of which ones are more volatile compared to the other.

Likewise, you have an understanding of which investment class will provide better rewards, but higher risks. Finding one that will be a good fit for your goals can be a challenge. But as you are starting out, low-risk and low-reward may not be such a bad idea as people make it out to be.

Because you're learning as you go. And once you are willing to take on a bit more risk, you can. That is as long as you have enough flexibility to make more riskier investments. Now that you know the basic concepts of investing, let's turn our focus now on how you can develop a strategy that works for you.

CHAPTER 4

Developing An Investing Strategy

An investing strategy can make the difference between being successful and losing out. In case of the latter, it may be due to a poor strategy or risk management (among other issues). Having a solid investing strategy can help you be able to achieve long-term success as an investor - whether you start in your teen years and continue onward into adulthood.

This chapter will go over how you can build an investing strategy that requires careful consideration of your investment objectives and risk tolerance. You'll also learn about the difference between short-term and long-term investing (along with the other key distinctions that may make them different).

Finally, you'll learn how you can adopt the mindset of being a young investor. Even if you are employing a strategy that works for you, having the mindset of an investor is very important. Because it will help you think from different perspectives about investing and how it all works.

We're just getting deeper into the fun of it all. Having an effective strategy does not guarantee profits. But it can help you hang onto your assets in the long-haul so you can enjoy the rewards.

Let's start now with how you can build an investing strategy from the ground up.

DEVELOPING YOUR INVESTMENT OBJECTIVES AND RISK TOLERANCE

One of the key aspects to building an investing strategy is developing your objectives and risk tolerance. Let's take a look now at how you can do this, step-by-step:

DETERMINE YOUR INVESTMENT OBJECTIVES

In other words, what are your investment goals? What do you want to achieve with them? These include wealth accumulation, retirement planning, funding your education, or saving up for something major to purchase.

This can be a car, a house, a luxury vacation, starting a business, or whatever you set your mind to. You need to clearly identify your objectives that will help guide you along your investment journey. Meanwhile, it is important that you stay focused in the long-term.

Your investment decisions can set you forward or set you back. At the end of the day, it's your call. Don't make your objectives vague, but rather clear, measurable, actionable, and realistic.

ASSESS YOUR TIME HORIZON

The time frame for you to achieve your investment goals should also be considered. Later on, we'll go into more detail about short-term and long-term. To begin, let's mention the time frames that separate the two.

Short-term goals are where something can happen anywhere from a period of five years or less. If you are looking to invest with short-term goals in mind, you will need to adopt a conservative strategy. In other words, you're going to be going after the low-risk, low-reward assets such as bonds.

Not to be outdone, ETFs and mutual funds can also be useful for a conservative investing strategy. And yes, even some stock trading can play into this as well.

Long-term goals pertain to something you want to achieve in a period of five to ten years or more. This includes but not limited to purchasing a home, retirement, or anything that you believe will occur much later in the future. In this instance, long-term goals can be good for those who want to utilize a more aggressive approach in their investing.

So if you are looking to achieve a long-term goal, you can get away with purchasing stocks or assets that will have its ups, downs, and sideways motions in the market. If you don't mind riding the waves for a long period of time, then this kind of strategy will be right up your alley.

Your time horizon will influence the type of assets that you invest in and the level of risk you can afford to take.

EVALUATE YOUR RISK TOLERANCE

Your risk tolerance involves understanding how comfortable you are with the ups and downs of the market. Some people may be willing to accept higher risks for potentially higher returns. Meanwhile, others may prefer a more conservative approach to minimize volatility.

Several factors that influence risk tolerance include age, financial situation, personal temperament, and investment knowledge. As a teenager, you might have a low risk tolerance given that you have never invested before. One more reason why you may want to consider a bit of a less than risky approach to investing until you are able to gain experience.

Not only that, you can also gain more capital as you are building up your wealth. And that will give you more than enough room to move onto slightly more risky investments if you want to. By that time you will be able to understand how investments work and which assets are considered more riskier than the other.

Your risk tolerance can increase with more experience. However, it never hurts to be a cautious investor for as long as you are investing your hard-earned money into assets that interest you.

DEFINE YOUR RISK TOLERANCE LEVEL

Once you understand risk tolerance as a whole, you can define the kind of investor you might be. What kind of risk tolerance do you have? Are you a conservative, moderate, or aggressive investor?

What are the differences between the three types? Let's take a look at the following:

- **Conservative investors:** A conservative investor will prioritize capital preservation and may focus on low-risk investments such as bonds or stocks that are stable and consistently pay dividends.

- **Moderate investors:** This is a balance between conservative and aggressive investing. You'll be diversifying your portfolio across different asset classes. In other words, a mix of low-risk and high-risk assets. Your portfolio will include stocks, bonds, and other assets that we'll mention when we discuss aggressive investing.

- **Aggressive investors:** For those that are seeking higher returns and willing to take on more risk, the aggressive approach will be more of their speed. This will include investing in stocks that are growth oriented. Even assets like cryptocurrency with its high level of volatility are considered to be good for aggressive investors. Emerging markets are also not an asset to overlook if you decided to go the aggressive route later on in life.

CONSIDER YOUR FINANCIAL SITUATION

Your current situation should be evaluated at this point. This includes your current income, expenses, savings, and existing assets. It will help you determine how much you can allocate to investments and how it aligns with your own objectives.

Don't forget that you also have an emergency fund that will be part of that situation as well. Then you have any possible debt that may exist. At this point in your life, debt may not be something to worry about as you might not have it.

That is unless you owe your parents (or someone else) for money. But nevertheless, carefully assess your financial situation as it will help become part of your investment strategy as you are starting out. The less debt and expenses you deal with, the more resources you can use for the purpose of investing.

DIVERSIFYING YOUR PORTFOLIO

No matter what your risk tolerance is, the important thing to do is diversify your portfolio. Not only is it one of the best strategies to manage risk, it also helps you sustain a total amount of returns across different assets. You can mix up different classes whether you are a conservative, moderate, or aggressive investor.

Every investor is different when it comes to their style of investing and what they include in their portfolio. Some will diversify but it will be all low-risk assets. Others will mix it up a bit with both low-risk and high-risk and others may be high-risk all the way.

Let's not forget that there is diversification based on industries, sectors, and geographical regions. Diversification will ensure that your portfolio doesn't take a huge hit whenever an asset has performed poorly.

This means having an asset that can offset that poor performer by doing good in whatever market it's in. For example, a poor performing stock can be offset by a call option that you have purchased on the same stock (an option is another investment asset, but it's an advanced one at best).

ASSESS YOUR INVESTMENT KNOWLEDGE

Your investment knowledge will be part of building an overall investing strategy. It's important that you be realistic about your investment knowledge. If you are a beginner, this will mean starting out with a low-cost investment option including ETFs and mutual funds.

Once you are able to become more comfortable with it, you can move onto individual stocks or more complex investment assets. Over time, your knowledge and expertise will get better.

As a teenager, you'll have plenty of time to build up that knowledge and expertise. You don't have to become a know-it-all investment guru. But enough to where you can make sound decisions on your investments and your overall future as a whole.

REVIEW AND ADJUST YOUR STRATEGY PERIODICALLY

Your investment strategy should give you enough flexibility to review it and make adjustments when and where applicable. Investing is a dynamic process and market conditions are subject to change over time. This means that you may need to make changes that need to stay aligned with your level of risk tolerance and financial objectives.

Be sure to re-balance your portfolio when necessary. Also, keep an eye out for any factors such as asset performance, changing market conditions, and evolving your financial situation.

Of course, professional advice can come in handy if you are stuck somewhere in your investment journey. It should also be a good idea to stay in the know about happenings around the investment landscape. This way, you can be able to make decisions based on your strategy at any time - even if it means making adjustments that stay in line with your goals.

LONG-TERM AND SHORT-TERM INVESTING: WHAT ARE THE DIFFERENCES?

There are plenty of differences between long-term and short-term investing. As mentioned, short-term pertains to goals that occur within a time frame of five years or less. Long-term will consist of goals that happen anywhere from more than five years to ten years (and beyond).

There are different key distinctions that we will be looking at. Let's provide you with them each with their own definitions of short-term and long-term:

TIME FRAME

- **Short-term investing:** Investors will hold onto investments for a brief period of time. This can include any time between a few days to a few months. The focus is taking advantage of any market fluctuations that happen in the short term or any specific events that can create profit opportunities.

- **Long-term investing:** This involves hanging onto investments for an extended period of time. This can range anywhere from a year, multiple years, or even decades. This will allow you to benefit from the potential growth and compounding of the investment over a specific period of time. This will allow the asset to appreciate and achieve for as long as their long-term financial goals exist.

INVESTMENT OBJECTIVES

- **Short-term investing:** Short-term investors often prioritize generating quick profits or capitalizing on short-term market movements. They might engage in strategies like day trading, swing trading, or event-based trading to exploit any short-term price volatility. The goal is to capitalize on short-term marketing inefficiencies rather than seeking long-term growth.

- **Long-term investing:** Long-term investors are focused on achieving specific financial objectives over an extended period, such as building wealth for education, retirement, or even financial independence. The emphasis is on capital appreciating and compounding returns over a period of time. Long-term investors will often employ strategies like buy-and-hold, dollar-cost averaging, and diversification to manage risk and achieve their long-term goals.

RISK AND VOLATILITY

- **Short-term investing:** There are higher levels of risk and volatility can be involved in the short-term. This can be due to the potential for sudden price fluctuations. Investors may need to closely monitor markets, analyze technical indicators, and react quickly to changing conditions. The time horizon, albeit short-term, increases the risk of losses if the market movements are unfavorable

- **Long-term investing:** This will be less focused on short-term market fluctuations. It will be more aligned with the overall growth potential of the investments. Volatility may still exist in a short-term time window. However, the longer time horizon will allow investors to ride out the market downturns while enjoying the benefit of overall uptrend of markets over time. Long-term investors will also enjoy being able to recover from market downturns over the course of time and capture long-term market returns in the process.

INVESTMENT SELECTION

- **Short-term investing:** Short-term investors will focus on individual stocks, currencies, and commodities. They may also focus on specific sectors with the potential for short-term price movements. Experienced investors may rely on technical analysis, market timing, or event-driven strategies in order to seek out any short-term opportunities.

- **Long-term investing:** Long-term investors will typically have a more diversified approach. They will have their investments spread across different asset classes like stocks, bonds, real estate, mutual funds, and ETFs among others. They may prioritize investments that align with long-term growth including blue chip stocks or index funds. Fundamental analysis will be more of their bread and butter compared to technical analysis along with the quality of the underlying asset.

Keep in mind that the distinction between long-term and short-term investing is not absolute. Some investors may incorporate the elements of both approaches into their own investment strategy. Once again, risk tolerance, individual goals, knowledge of investment, and time pertaining to active management will play a role in determining either a short-term or long-term approach.

ADOPTING THE MINDSET OF A YOUNG INVESTOR

As a young investor starting out, it is important to develop a mindset of an investor that can be successful. There are elements that will help you build one from the ground up. Here's what they are:

EMBRACE A LONG-TERM PERSPECTIVE

You must realize that time is your biggest asset. You will take advantage of it by focusing on long-term goals and investing with a horizon over several decades. You'll understand that investing is a journey and the assets you invest in will experience ups and downs along the way.

Be sure to stay committed to your long-term strategy and avoid making impulsive decisions based on short-term market fluctuations.

CULTIVATE PATIENCE AND DISCIPLINE

They say that patience is a virtue. That is the case when it comes to investing. It is essential to resist the temptation of chasing quick profits or constantly switching back and forth from one investment to another. Especially if it's making short-term market movements.

Stay disciplined and stick with your investment plan. You must never let your emotions get to you when it comes to the volatility of the market. Contribute your investments on a regular basis and trust in the power of compounding to work for you.

EDUCATE YOURSELF

Investing can be a complex thing. But you can take the time to educate yourself over a period of time. Be sure to follow any financial publications that are reliable and take advantage of any online resources that will help you build up your investment knowledge.

Of course, reading books on investing won't hurt either. We are all lifelong learners, even if we've long graduated school. Continuous learning about investing can help you make better decisions while navigating the markets.

START EARLY AND BE CONSISTENT

With time being a significant advantage, it can really help you in the long run. The sooner you start, the longer your investments will have to grow. Even if you can contribute a small amount at the outset, being consistent with investing is essential.

Automate regular contributions to your investment accounts, if possible. This includes setting up automatic transfers from your bank account. This consistency will allow you to benefit from dollar-cost averaging, which will allow you to purchase more shares at lower prices and fewer shares if the prices are high. This can help bring down your average cost per share over a period of time.

IT's OK TO TAKE CALCULATED RISKS

A young investor has plenty of time to recover from potential losses and can afford to take on a certain level of risk. Consider allocating a portion of your portfolio to higher-risk investments like stocks or growth-oriented assets when you have a little bit of experience under your belt.

But remember, risk tolerance should align with your investment decisions. And yes, don't forget to make sure that diversifying your portfolio is a plus. Especially when you want to mitigate as much risk as possible.

BE MINDFUL OF FEES AND EXPENSES

Fees and expenses associated with your investments are something that you need to pay attention to. Fees that are too high can eat into your returns over time.

That is why it is important to consider low-cost investment options. Meanwhile, minimize other expenses so it can allow you to maximize the compounding effect of your investments. Also, look for any fees and expenses that you might be charged on a regular basis if you are looking for a reliable online broker for all of your investment needs.

STAY ADAPTABLE AND OPEN TO LEARNING

The investment landscape is always changing. What might work today may not work tomorrow. So it is important to stay adaptable and open to new ideas and investment opportunities.

Meanwhile, be sure to evaluate your investment strategy and make the necessary adjustments. Also, make sure that you learn from any of your investment experience (and even the experience of others). Building wealth is a long-term process and adopting the mindset of a learner will help you make better decisions going forward when it comes to investments.

BOTTOM LINE

The great thing about an investment strategy is that it can help you make better decisions. You'll know when to get in and out of an investment that you've put your money in. You now understand the differences between short-term and long-term as far as different elements are concerned like time frame and risk/volatility.

Finally, adopting the mindset of a young investor is important. Be sure to utilize the principles that make such a mindset more than possible to develop. When you do, you'll look at investing from a different perspective.

Over time, you'll see things from a different angle. You will know when a good investment opportunity is there and one where you need to steer clear from for whatever reason.

Without a proper investing strategy, it would be having a car without the engine. Or it would be like flying blind into the fog with no place to go. The last thing you need is for your investing endeavors to come to an end before they begin due to the lack of an investing strategy.

CHAPTER 5

Stocks and Mutual Funds/ETFs: Everything You Need To Know

Finally, we get to discuss more about some of the all important assets for investors. These include stocks, mutual funds and ETFs. We have touched on bonds and other assets for a bit throughout the book.

However, we believe that for young investors - stocks will be mostly one of the major assets they'll focus on at the start of their experience. This chapter will discuss everything you need to know about stocks, mutual funds, and ETFs. We'll go into detail about the assets along with the pros and cons.

Afterwards, we'll make a comparison of the three so you have a good idea of what makes them different from one another. Buckle up - because this is going to be a fun ride for you. Let's get started right now.

THE PURPOSE OF STOCKS AND HOW THEY OPERATE

The stock market is a platform where individuals and organizations can buy and sell shares of publicly traded companies. It serves as a marketplace for investors to trade securities like stocks and bonds. Understanding how the stock market works involves grasping the purpose of stocks and the mechanics behind their operation.

In case you may have forgotten, let's explain what a stock is once again. When a company is publicly traded, they issue stocks. This will divide the ownership into shares.

Each share represents a portion of the company's ownership and the individuals that purchase these will become shareholders. As a shareholder, you have several benefits that are afforded to both companies and investors. A company issuing the stock will provide the opportunity to raise capital in order to fund their operations.

They also will be able to expand their business or invest in new ventures. By selling these shares, the company is giving investors the chance to become partial owners and participate in the company's growth and profits.

Stocks offer the potential for capital appreciation and income in the form of dividends, which means they can earn an amount of money depending on the number of shares they hold. For example, if a company offers a dividend of $1 per share and you hold onto 100, you get $100 in total dividends - which can be paid on an annual basis.

Some companies will pay dividends to stockholders based on a certain period of time. However, not all companies are created equal when it comes to the frequency of the dividends and how much is paid per share. Dividends are perfect for an additional income stream and can be used to reinvest for more shares.

If a company performs well and its value increases, the price of the stock will rise. An investor will have the opportunity to sell their shares at a profit.

The operation of the stock market involves the interaction between buyers and sellers. Buyers or investors or traders will purchase stock that they believe will increase in value. Sellers may want to sell their shares for whatever reason necessary.

One of the main reasons is that they are selling it at a high enough price. They may have bought the shares at a lower price and are selling it at a higher one.

The stock market will facilitate the transaction through exchanges. In the United States, it's the New York Stock Exchange (NYSE) or the NASDAQ. Buyers and sellers will place orders to buy or sell stocks, specifying the desired amount and the price that they are willing to pay.

When the market matches these orders and when a buyer and seller agrees on a price - a trade occurs. Stock prices will be influenced by a variety of factors. These include the financial performance of the company, industry trends, economic conditions, and investor sentiment. The forces of supply and demand in the stock market determine the price at which shares are bought and sold.

Like any other investment opportunity, the stock market carries risks. The stock prices can be volatile and can rise and fall based on several different factors. They include but are not limited to market conditions, geopolitical events, and company-specific news.

As such, an investor must conduct research and diversify their portfolio. They also must also consider their risk tolerance before investing in stocks.

WHAT TYPE OF STOCKS ARE TRADED ON THE MARKET?

There are several different types of stocks that are traded on the stock market. They are categorized based on the various factors - including the rights and privileges that they offer to shareholders, the size and nature of the companies they represent, and their potential for capital appreciation and dividends.

These are the stocks that are traded on the stock market:

COMMON STOCKS

This is the most prevalent type of stocks that are traded on the market. When people refer to stocks in general, this is the kind of stock that it is referred to. Common stockholders will possess voting rights in the company and may receive dividends if the company distributes them.

In the event of a liquidation, common stockholders will have a lower claim on the assets compared to those who are preferred stockholders or bondholders.

PREFERRED STOCKS

Preferred stocks have characteristics of both stocks and bonds. A preferred stockholder will have a higher claim on the company assets and earnings compared to their common stockholder counterparts. In the event of a liquidation, preferred stockholders will have priority over them.

One of the things they do not have is voting rights - which is something that common stockholders do.

BLUE-CHIP STOCKS

A blue-chip stock represents shares of a large, well-established company with a history of stable earnings and a strong market presence. These companies are often industry leaders and have a reputation for reliability and consistent performance.

Blue-chip stocks are typically considered less volatile and are the favorites among conservative investors looking for long-term stability.

GROWTH STOCKS

Growth stocks are shares of a company that are expected to grow at an above-average rate compared to the overall market. These companies reinvest their earnings to expand their operations, develop new products, or enter new markets.

Growth stocks will generally not pay any substantial dividends since the focus is on reinvesting in the future growth of the company (hence the name). Investors who believe in the growth potential of the company will often invest in the growth stocks with the exception of capital appreciation.

VALUE STOCKS

Value stocks are shares of companies that are considered undervalued by the market. These companies typically have solid fundamentals. Yet, their stock prices might not reflect their intrinsic value due to several reasons like temporary market trends, investor sentiment, or overlooked potential.

Value investors seek out these stocks with the anticipation that the market will eventually recognize the company's true worth and expect the stock price to rise.

SMALL-CAP, MID-CAP, AND LARGE-CAP STOCKS

Stocks are categorized based on their market capitalization or their "market cap". There are three different types of cap stocks: small, mid, and large. Let's break down how these stocks are categorized by their market capitalization:

- **Large-cap:** These are companies with a market capitalization of $10 billion to $200 billion.

- **Mid-cap:** Market capitalization of $2 billion to $10 billion

- **Small-cap:** Market capitalization of $300 million to $2 billion

The way the market cap is calculated is when the share price is multiplied by the amount of outstanding shares. For example, if a company has a hundred million outstanding shares being sold at $20 a share, that equals out to $2 billion - making it a mid-cap stock.

Get the idea now? Keep in mind that the classification of these stocks will fall into these categories, giving investors a sense of how large the company is, its growth potential, and its risk profile.

WHAT ARE THE PROS AND CONS OF STOCK TRADING?

Let's take a look now at the pros and cons of investing in the stock market:

PROS

- **Potential for capital appreciation:** You can make profit based on the increased price of a stock. You can purchase it at one price and sell it higher.

- **Dividend income:** Some, but not all stocks will pay dividends to their shareholders. These are a portion of the company's profits that are distributed to the investors. Dividend stocks may be one of the best options for young investors as they can provide a regular income stream. You can be an income-focused investor and take advantage of these dividends. Another way you can use them is by reinvesting it into more shares, giving you a much larger piece of the company.

- **Portfolio diversification:** Investing in the stock market allows you to diversify your investment portfolio. By spreading your investments across different stocks, sectors, and asset classes, you can reduce the risk associated with having all of your eggs in one basket. Of course, you already know that diversification will be helpful in softening the impact of any losses that may occur.

- **Accessibility and liquidity:** The stock market is generally accessible to individual investors. It offers them a level playing field for all participants. Buying and selling stocks is relatively easy thanks to the availability of online brokerage platforms. Stocks are considered liquid investments, meaning you can usually share them quickly and convert them into cash.

CONS OF STOCK MARKET INVESTING

VOLATILITY AND RISK

The stock market is inherently volatile. The stock prices can fluctuate in response to numerous factors. The potential for high returns may exist, but not without a higher level of risk. Which means you may risk losing some, if not all of your invested capital if the companies you invest in all perform poorly or face financial difficulty.

EMOTIONAL IMPACT

Stock market investing can invoke emotions like fear and greed. This can lead to irrational decision-making. An investor may panic and sell during a market downturn or get overly optimistic and buy at the peak of a market cycle.

Allowing your emotions to take over can lead to a negative impact on your entire investment experience. Which means that you could negatively impact the returns you are due to receive and hinder your long-term financial goals in the process.

LACK OF CONTROL

As a shareholder, you have limited control over the day-to-day operations and decision-making of the companies you invest in. Even if you own a significant number of shares, you won't have overall control over the overall direction and management of the company.

So no, you don't have the authority to hire or fire anyone. Probably a good thing, if you think about it. But nevertheless, you have voting rights to help with some of the company's decisions that they need to make.

However, this lack of control means that your investment returns will depend on the performance of the company and its management. So if the company fails, you will have no fault to deal with. But you will lose money depending on the amount you invested into the company.

REGULATORY AND EXTERNAL FACTORS

The stock market operates within a regulatory framework. Changes in regulations or government policies can impact the market and individual stocks. These factors include economic recessions, political instability, or unexpected events that can affect the stock price and the sentiment of the market.

MUTUAL S FUNDS AND ETFs

Now, we're going to take a look at mutual funds and exchange-traded funds (ETFs). These are an excellent option for new investors since they won't need any direct management. They are professionally managed, making it easier for beginners like yourself.

Both of these pool money from multiple investors to invest in a variety of assets. This will provide investors with benefits of diversification and professional management. Now, let's do an individual breakdown of both mutual funds and ETFs.

MUTUAL FUNDS

Structure

Mutual funds are investment assets that are managed by professional fund managers. They issue shares to investors and the money is collected to purchase a diversified portfolio of securities. These can be actively managed or passively managed (as index funds).

Diversification

Mutual funds offer instant diversification by investing in a broad range of assets. These can include stocks, bonds, and money market assets. This will help you reduce the risk associated with individual securities.

Pricing and trading

Mutual funds are priced at the net asset value (NAV) per share, which is calculated at the end of each trading day. Mutual fund shares can be bought or sold at the NAV price. The transactions are processed once a day after the closure of the market.

Costs

Mutual funds may have various costs. These include management fees, administrative expenses, and sales loads (front-end or back-end fees). These costs can impact the overall returns.

Investment minimums

Mutual funds might have minimum investment requirements. They can vary depending on the fund. Some of these funds offer lower minimums for retirement accounts or subsequent investments.

Distribution

Mutual funds may distribute dividends and capital gains to shareholders, typically on a regular basis. Investors can choose to reinvest these distributions or receive them in cash.

ETFs

Structure

ETFs are investment funds that are traded on the stock exchange. These are similar to individual stocks. They are designed to track the performance of an underlying index or asset class. These can be passively managed or actively managed.

Diversification

ETFs will offer broad diversification by replicating the composition and performance of an underlying index or asset class. They hold a basket of securities that mirror the index that they track.

Pricing and Trading

ETFs are traded throughout the trading day on the stock exchanges. The price of an ETF share may differ from its underlying net asset value (NAV) due to market forces.

Costs

ETFs generally have lower expense ratios compared to mutual funds. They may also be subject to brokerage commissions and bid-ask spreads when buying or selling shares.

Investment minimums

ETFs typically have no minimum investment requirements, allowing investors to buy as few or as many shares as they desire.

Tax efficiency

ETFs are structured in a way that allows for greater tax efficiency compared to mutual funds. They generate fewer taxable events due to their unique creation and redemption process.

KEY SIMILARITIES BETWEEN ETFs AND MUTUAL FUNDS

Diversification

Both mutual funds and ETFs offer diversification by investing in a basket of securities. This reduces the impact of individual holdings on the overall investment.

Professional management

Both investment assets are managed by professionals who make investment decisions on behalf of the investors.

Regulatory oversight

Mutual funds and ETFs are subject to regulatory oversight and must adhere to a set of rules and regulations. They are designed to protect the investors.

SELECTING THE RIGHT ETFs/MUTUAL FUNDS FOR YOUR FINANCIAL GOALS

Selecting the right ETFs or mutual funds that align with your financial goals is essential. Here are come considerations that you need to look over:

- Your definitive financial goals

- Asset allocation

- Investment strategy

- Research and due diligence

- Performance and risk

- Expense ratios and fees

- Diversification and funds holding

- Track record and fund management

- Tax efficiency

- Professional advice if needed

Selecting an ETF or mutual fund can be a process that can take some time. Yet, it is important to consider these factors before you select one that is aligned with your financial goals.

WHAT ARE THE PROS AND CONS OF ETFs AND MUTUAL FUNDS?

In this section, we're going to separate ETFs and mutual funds when we provide you with a list of their own pros and cons. To begin, let's list off the ones for ETFs:

ETF PROS

- **Diversification:** Allows you to hold on to different assets for more risk adversity

- **Trading flexibility:** Allows you to trade during the day and use various types of orders

- **Lower expense ratios:** These are lower compared to their managed mutual fund counterparts. ETFs follow a passive investment strategy and aim to replicate the performance of an index.

- **Tax efficiency:** ETFs tend to be more tax-efficient compared to mutual funds. The unique structure of ETFs allow for potential tax advantages, such as in-kind creation and redemption, which can help minimize capital gains distributions.

- **Transparency:** ETFs disclose their holdings on a daily basis, allowing investors to know exactly what securities they own. This transparency can help investors make better decisions.

ETF CONS

- **Trading costs:** ETFs may offer flexibility, but investors may incur commission or bid-ask spreads when they buy or sell the shares. Frequent trading can also lead to an increase in trading costs.

- **Premiums and discounts:** The price of an ETF can deviate from its NAV due to market forces. Investors may buy shares at a premium or sell at a discount to the underlying asset value.

- **Limited control:** ETF investors do not have control over the individual securities within the fund. They are dependent on the fund manager's investment decisions - which may not align with their specific preferences.

- **Availability of certain asset classes:** Some of the less liquid asset classes may have limited ETF options available. This can restrict investors' access to certain investment opportunities.

MUTUAL FUND PROS

- **Professional management:** Mutual funds are managed by professional fund managers. They will make the investment decisions on behalf of the investors. This will be beneficial to those who are new to investing or would like a hands-off approach.

- **Variety of investment strategies:** Mutual funds will offer a wide range of investment strategies. This will give investors the power to choose funds that align with their specific objectives and risk tolerances.

- **Accessibility:** Mutual funds are typically available through various investment platforms and can be easily purchased or redeemed at the end of the day NAV price.

- **Automatic reinvestment:** Many mutual funds will offer automatic reinvestment of dividends and capital gains. This will allow investors to compound their returns over time.

- **Potential for active management:** Actively managed mutual funds have the potential to outperform their benchmark if the fund manager's decisions are successful.

MUTUAL FUND CONS

- **Higher expense ratios:** Mutual funds generally have higher expense ratios compared to ETFs. The costs associated with active management, research, and administration are passed on to investors, potentially impacting overall returns.

- **Capital gains distribution:** Mutual funds are required to distribute realized capital gains to shareholders. These can be taxable for the investors, whether they sold the fund shares or not.

- **Limited trading flexibility:** Mutual funds are priced and traded at the end of each trading day at the NAV. Which means the investors won't be able to buy or sell the shares at intra-day prices.

- **Lack of transparency:** Periodically, mutual funds will disclose their holdings. This will typically happen on a quarterly basis. This can make it more challenging for investors who are interested in tracking the current holdings and potential changes.

STOCKS VS MUTUAL FUNDS/ETFS A COMPARISON

Before we wrap up the chapter, let's give you an overview-style comparison of each asset. Let's begin with stocks:

- Individual ownership will be for individual stocks. There's a good chance that you might not have this luxury with mutual funds or ETFs

- Potential for high returns exist. And for this reason, stocks will be riskier compared to their ETF/mutual fund counterparts. A stock will have concentrated exposure to a company or sector.

- Stocks require thorough research, analysis, and monitoring of each individual company. This includes looking over financial statements, analyzing market trends, and assessing competitive factors.

- Building a diversified portfolio of individual stocks can be more challenging and time-consuming. This will require the careful selection of stocks across different sectors and asset classes in order to mitigate risk.

- With ETFs/Mutual funds, diversification is basically done for you.

- ETFs/Mutual funds are professionally managed.

- All ETFs/mutual funds have lower transaction costs

- Simplified investing is provided by ETFs and mutual funds, but not stocks

- ETFs/mutual funds are typically accessible to individual investors since they offer a low minimum investment requirement compared to individual stocks. Therefore, it's a better option for new investors - including teenagers that are interested in investing themselves.

Simply put, if you are a teenager interested in investing - the option is quite clear. As you are starting out, ETFs/mutual funds might be the perfect option. Not to mention, it will be the best entry level asset that will help you understand the movements of the market, how investing works, and the level of challenges you face when compared to trading individual stocks and building a portfolio of them.

Not to mention, the costs will be cheaper compared to individual stocks. If you want to invest but don't have a lot of money to work with, ETF/Mutual funds may be the best option to start with.

BOTTOM LINE

Stocks, mutual funds, and ETFs are some of the most popular investments out there for new investors. As you start out, consider mutual funds and ETFs as your best option. This will give you a solid understanding of some of the aspects of investing.

This includes diversification, selection of stocks, how they are managed, and much more. When you gain more experience, you will start to dabble in individual stocks. From there, you'll be able to understand the concepts of building a portfolio of diverse assets that can give you excellent returns over a period of time.

CONCLUSION

Becoming A Confident Investor

There you have it. We have reached the conclusion. We hope that you have learned a wealth of information on how you can invest as a teenager.

Just a friendly reminder that you have an attached bonus that came with the book. It is a list of brokers that allow custodial accounts along with other educational resources you can check out. Use that to your advantage as you continue along your journey as an investor.

So, let's recap everything that you have learned throughout this book:

FINANCIAL LITERACY IS APPRECIATED - BUT NOT REQUIRED

Earlier in the book, we stated that financial literacy is not a prerequisite for investing. However, we highly appreciate that you learn a basic amount of it before you consider investing. At the same time, it's important to instill the basic practices of personal finance as well.

This includes being able to set a budget, understanding income and expenses, and setting up an emergency fund among others. The thing to be aware of is that financial literacy is a skill that can certainly help you navigate through all the financial situations - great and small.

You'll be able to understand the basics of personal finance and beyond. At this point, we hope you've made a plan to follow a budget and even begin saving. If you haven't already, take your time - there is no rush.

KNOW YOUR LEVEL OF RISK TOLERANCE

Not everyone will have the same level of risk tolerance as you do. As you start out, it will be low. However, it will build up over time with experience.

From there, you can decide how much more risk you are willing to take. Some may even stay within a certain comfort zone because it may be in line with their own financial goals. And that's fine if you feel that way as well.

It's OK to up the risk tolerance a bit if you so choose. However, make sure you have the experience beforehand. It's never a good idea to try and start off with high-risk investments.

That's like diving into the deep end of a swimming pool and you don't know how to swim. You'll be in big trouble if you do. Not to mention, it's quite unsafe.

So it would be ideal for you to learn how to start from the bottom and work your way upward. It may be hard to determine what your ceiling is in terms of risk tolerance. But getting experience is the best way to build it up.

EACH ASSET HAS THEIR OWN LEVELS OF RISK AND REWARD

Low-risk equals low-reward. And high-risk equals high-reward. That can't be put together simply enough. You want to be able to learn which assets will be less risky compared to the other.

At some point, your portfolio just might have a mix of both. And that is something that you might like. Of course, we do appreciate diversification - whether it's a mix of low-risk and high-risk assets.

But remember, it doesn't have to be like that at all. Diversification can be different low-risk, low-reward assets. Or if you want to be really bold - it can be all high-risk and high-reward (we probably don't recommend that for obvious reasons).

YOUR FINANCIAL GOALS ARE NOT THE SAME AS OTHERS

Your financial goals are unique. You have an idea of what they look like. Or how you want them to look in the long-term.

Some may have short-term goals. Others may have long-term ones. The difference is that there may be different durations.

Someone may want to meet theirs within five years. Others in ten years or beyond that. The point is that everyone has financial goals with different timelines, intents, and purposes.

Try not to duplicate other people's financial goals. Focus on yours and yours alone. And by the way, people tend to achieve their financial goals at their own pace.

Don't be ashamed that you're going slower than others. And don't forget - setbacks happen. They can throw you a bit off course and distract you.

The best part is to keep going. After all, you still have plenty of time to recover from the losses and setbacks that may occur along the way.

WORDS OF ENCOURAGEMENT AND TIPS FOR ONGOING SUCCESS

For the final part of this book, we'll leave you with some words of encouragement and tips for ongoing success. It's up to you to take these to heart. Here's what we want to share with you:

USE YOUR TIME WISELY

Take your time and spend it wisely on your investment journey. This includes researching the assets you are interested in investing. Or talking to a financial professional about your goals.

Use that time to assess your financial success in investing. And determine whether or not any adjustments are necessary. Try not to rush into everything.

As the old fable goes - slow and steady wins the race. And with the time advantage you have, that saying is proven to be true.

IT'S OK TO HAVE LOSSES

Every investor in the world has dealt with losses. If anyone who has succeeded in the market said that they never experienced them - that's a lie. You will deal with losses and so will other investors.

It is important to handle them in the best way possible. Keep the emotions out of it. Think ahead to the future.

Accept the fact that it's all part of the process. When you do this, that will put you ahead of those who try to use investing the wrong way. While they give up in frustration, you stay on with the knowledge that you will reach your financial goals sooner or later.

DON'T BE AFRAID TO TAKE CALCULATED RISKS

This includes checking on whether or not you can up your risk tolerance. After spending time investing in ETFs, consider taking on the challenge of stocks. You have a good idea of how they all work.

So why not give it a shot? You might enjoy building your portfolio with them. Calculated risks are a lot better than the risks that people take such as going 'all in' and trying to let it ride. That risk is uncalculated and it will cause an investor to lose it all.

CONTINUE TO LEARN ABOUT INVESTING

Life is an ongoing learning process. The same can be said about investing. With everything changing every day, there may be a new way to invest.

As we have said earlier, what may work today may not work tomorrow. So be prepared to learn when necessary. And adjust and adapt when it's needed.

We hope that you have enjoyed reading this book. A ton of awesome information has gone into this. And we hope that you are using the actionable steps that will help you achieve investment success.

We wish you all the best in your financial endeavors - whatever they may be.

LIST OF CUSTODIAL ACCOUNTS FOR INVESTING

Even though you can invest as a teen, there are stock trading platforms that won't allow persons under the age of 18 to open up their own account. If this is the case, this is where a custodial account will come in handy.

We have taken the liberty of including a list of the following online platforms. These will offer custodial accounts for those who want to trade ETFs, Mutual Funds, or even stocks. We'll also include any additional information that will apply to the one you intend to use.

We will also make sure that these have minimum fees and account minimums (when starting out). Let's take a look at the following list below:

CHARLES SCHAWB

Charles Schawb has been one of the most trusted names in the investment industry for many years. A custodial account is available through them and you can trade stocks, ETFs, and mutual funds. While there is an account minimum of $0, there are some premium accounts like Intelligent Portfolios that require an account minimum of $5000.

While there are no fees for the intelligent portfolios, its upgraded version Intelligent Portfolios Premium has a $30 per month fee.

The app is compatible with both iPhone and Android. Which means you can make trades any time (during trading hours) and any place.

While there are plenty of trading platforms with their own apps for trading, this one is user friendly (and for good reason).

VANGUARD

This offers ETFs, mutual funds, and stocks. The account minimum is $0 but is higher for accounts with advisor services. Likewise, the fees for regular accounts are $0.

If you choose to have your portfolio professionally managed, there is a fee ranging from 0.20 to 0.30 percent.

Vanguard offers commission-free trades for stocks and ETFs. You can also get access to mutual funds that are low-cost. If you are serious about retirement (or investing to build up your retirement fund), this might be the best option for both teens and adults.

FIDELITY INVESTMENTS

No fees, no account minimum, no problem (with a standard account, of course). You get plenty of investment types with Fidelity Investments. This is an excellent choice for those who want to invest in the long-term.

You'll have plenty of research tools to work with should you decide to do a little technical analysis.

MERRILL LYNCH

Another venerable trading platform that has been around for years. If you are considering guided investing, this one has a minimum of $1000 - one of the lowest on the market. But if you can handle it yourself, there's no need to pay for a minimum.

One of the best things about this platform is that it gives you 24/7 customer service via live chat. If you or your parents have a Bank of America account, it can be linked to your Merrill Lynch custodial account.

TD AMERITRADE

If you are looking for multiple apps for different trading goals, this may be a good option. You can have free commissions on stocks and ETFs. It's even got plenty of research and educational resources at your disposal if you need it.

There is robo-advice and managed portfolios, but they will come at a much higher price point. You can trade on your smartphone using their dedicated app.

E*TRADE

If you are looking for low-cost automated investing, you'll need a minimum balance of $500. If you don't have enough for Merril Lynch's Guided investing, this is another option. Otherwise, you can do it yourself without having to pony up a lot for a minimum amount to get started.

There are a large number of no-load, no-fee mutual funds that are also available. Even better, you have 24/7 support and plenty of online and mobile offerings - which are competitive compared to other platforms.

Made in United States
Orlando, FL
07 June 2024

47603213R10055